Sycamore
and Other Poems

Sycamore
and Other Poems

Randall Mawer

Writers Club Press
San Jose New York Lincoln Shanghai

Sycamore and Other Poems

Writers Club Press
an imprint of iUniverse.com, Inc.

For information address:
iUniverse.com, Inc.
5220 S 16th, Ste. 200
Lincoln, NE 68512
www.iuniverse.com

Four "other poems" have appeared in *Fantasque*

ISBN: 0-595-14654-6

Printed in the United States of America

Contents

Sycamore

For though we must pause not a moment in the narrative we may here hastily note that all his images at this time were simple in the extreme to match his senses and were mostly taken from things he had liked the taste of as a boy. But if his senses were simple they were at the same time extremely strong.

—Virginia Woolf, *Orlando*

❧ *The Pond*

Lunker bass haunt Geary's Pond, or did,
Thousands of days ago, when we were old,
Old with wisdom, old with love's certainty,
Love unconditional, or no love, no,
No love at all,
                when a spring-fed pond
Spang in the middle of ten acres of beans,
Colder than sin, deeper than it was wide,
Clear, clear to the bottom, where weeds slow danced
And hid the bass we knew were there, called.

And we, drawn, hurdling the rows of green,
Shucking our clothes as we leaped, crusted with dust
Or weltered in sweat and stable muck, thought
Not at all of miles or days but just of *now!*
And flew, legs peddling, far, far up and out,
Hanging in air, in time, above earth's eye,
Sky mirror, summer's core, boys' secret.

No doubt because he was sickly, angry,
Ugly, Ronnie Esterhaus was never missed
When absent, seen when present, truly mourned
When gone. Did we even know he shadowed us
That day, see him dive, guess the cause of roil
And bubble above entangling weeds?
We were not sure, and talked about it
Almost not at all, quieted not by guilt
But by unsureness, by memory's lies,

If lies they were, by premonition—
Could it be?—of ten thousand days and more
Treading water still cold but clear no longer.

❧ *Social*

Late spring, and the ice cream social rolls round
Yet again, with dusty trestle tables
Passed to the tune of barely swallowed oaths
Up and out of the church's cellar way
While chickens simmer and fall off their bones
In certain select kitchens. Lights are strung
From trees and tested. The Omar man brings
Racks and racks of buns. By midafternoon
The ice cream crew starts cranking and smoking,
Turn, turn about.
     Mrs. VonBlon's ladies
Are manufacturing spaetzle for soup
(All that chicken broth!) in the parsonage,
And outside of town Mrs. Hosterman
Grates longhorn for what will be her chewy
Gooey golden macaroni and cheese.
The lemonade (fresh, by the washtub full)
Is a-making,
    and there will be hot dogs
And pies, oh, pies, plump and lattice crusted,
Peach, cherry, apple, and is that rhubarb?

Poet and Peasant will suffer alike
At the hands of the school band. (Sousa will
Fare better.) Uncharacteristic prayers
For no rain will be answered. The organ
Fund will fatten, as will the folk at large,
Recipes will change hands, the laughter at
The washing-up sinks in the church kitchen

Will ring unseemly loud
                        as the late breeze
Bumps the wee lights which in their turn will cast
Tree shadows on the lawn. Car doors will thump,
True night descend, and the last cat abroad
Claim the whole of Sycamore for its own.

❧ *George Hannum*

George Hannum kept beer under the bulk tank
In the milk-house, long neck Pabsts when all such
Bottles were long necked, and a shelf of poems
Over it: Goldsmith, Gray, Longfellow, Watts—
George wanted cadence in his head, constant,
Like the solid plod of his best Holsteins
Finding the barn, morning and eve, deepening
The path without widening it, udders
Heavy and swaying, eyes mild, each knowing
Her own name, her stanchion, her place in line.

George Hannum hunted squirrels with a rifle,
A muzzle loader his grand-dad bequeathed
To the only one who wanted it, George.
You found a likely clearing before dawn,
Feeling your way, showing no light, quiet,
And awaited the sunrise and the squirrels,
Which arrived together. Shot in the eye,
This game made good meat. George liked that long gun,
Cleaned it when he didn't need to. His boy,
A bad apple, said George liked it too well,
Better than him, the boy that is, and George
Allowed the claim. Said the rifle never
Failed him in a tight place… unlike the boy,
He might have finished but didn't need to.

Because George Hannum grew up driving teams
He grasped the notion of tandem pulling.

He hated chickens, brainless and noisy,
His wife's included, but she managed them,
He would have had to say, had anyone
Asked, right, and the egg money was steady.
As a regular thing, at supper, George
Inquired if she needed anything, and
He never, no not ever, begrutched her
Her stake for bingo, Friday nights in town.

George Hannum had a friend, a Methodist,
The minister, in fact, at his wife's church.
They hunted together sometimes, pheasant,
And if a bird flushed and dropped when both shot
Reverend Coleman always yelled, "I got him!"
Like that God of his, George thought, forever
Claiming, nodding as if He knew something
You didn't know, smiling, giving away
What wasn't His to give.
                         Thus George Hannum,
Slapping Delilah's rump, the last beast out,
Snapping the cap off the night's first Pabst and
Reviewing his day, his theology.
When the path took a familiar turn and
Disclosed a vista George had seen before,
He took down Isaac Watts's sacred songs,
Odd choice for the town skeptic, to be sure.

❧ *Foy Town Road*

The road south slid round the rocky shoulder
Of what would become Cemetery Hill
When its first dead made Sycamore a town
With a past, this before the railroads and
The churches and the grain elevator,
To be seen for miles, taller, much taller than
The tallest trees, church spires, water tower.
Old Town flanked the track between hill and ford,
And there, across these same shallows, they built,
In time, the first bridge, and the road rested
Awhile along the creek and then essayed
The long southbound grade, becoming Main Street.

Back at the bridge, the merest path went straight
Up a steepening slope, through waste ground, toward
Foy Town, home of the shiftless and ill clad
Since someone knew who Foy was. In between,
The track cut deep and deeper into clay,
And scrub woods overhung the way through tracts
Where sand and brambles and broken fences
Made chaos visible. Here random rocks
Sprang up in the road, angling at axle
And oil pan, and dogs on urgent errands
Ran, noses down, twixt banks pitted with caves.

Through a special thicket beside this lane
Rose an elm, lightning blasted, grape-vine swathed,
Where, high up and haughty, a red-tailed hawk
Clutched the same branch the daylight clock around,

Counting rabbits on the opposite slope,
Tracing the trails of mice, dreaming hawk dreams.
He could not remember views from elsewhere,
Did not anticipate a move, till lunch;
Thus, for the moment, he was eternal,
And if he marked the woman stringing beans
On the back porch of the hilltop house there,
Off to the west, it was not to wonder
What she would do next or what perplexed her.
She, for her part, did not, indeed could not
See the hawk at all, though her glance crossed his
From time to time, piqued by a sometime sheen,
Quick water threading the dark woods below.

❧ *Mary and Margaret*

There were no girls in Sycamore, at all.
Boys abounded, swarmed the alleys, friends
To be loitered with, traveled with, strangers
To dance with, you and they like tom cats,
Arched, stiff legged, and circling a common point.
Boys tapped at windows, hung from trees, edged
Round corners, whistled—sharp or debonair.
Boys rode bikes, threw fits, went home to Mommy.
But girls? What girls were there? none! where? no
    where!
No, I tell a lie. The Heffernan twins,
Mary and Margaret, they were there,
On their own front walk, laid out for hopscotch
Neatly, in multi-colored pastel chalk,
Licking the lard out of Hydroxes or
Skipping rope, prettily, and talking code.
Their outfits—I see blue-and-white checked
    jumpers—
Matched. Bits of the same cloth tipped their pigtails,
Blond. They showed no smidgin of interest
In where we were going. And soon they moved
Out of Sycamore and into my dreams.

❧ *Tippy*

Tippy was a black and brown shepherd cross,
Crossed with what?—collie maybe—no one knew,
Smallish, not real bright, a perpetual
Vulpine grin on his face. Gran loved that dog,
Loved him with the worthiest sort of love,
Unreasonable. For Tippy bit tires,
Killed chickens, got tangled often with skunks
And bigger dogs. Look people in the eye
Tip could not do but tucked his clumsy tale
Away, sidled, whined, snapped air, and was gone.

Tippy walked out with Gran every evening
After supper, when, light or dark, she hiked
To the end of the paved road, to the house,
Empty then, gone now, where she had been born.
Tippy walked out with Gran, but never back,
Sensing always something, a smell, a twitch
Or shift in the hedgerow, of more interest
Than Gran with her memories, and promptly
Betraying her as she never would him.

Grampa was in the barn when he heard screams
Like roof tin tearing, knew that that damned dog
Had chased one car too many, grabbed up bags
And a surcingle for strapping and ran.
Gran was already there, holding Tippy,
Snapping and bloody, in her lap and arms.
"Best let me put him down, Lucille," he said,
But Gran regarded him in just that way

And he phoned for the vet, who came quickly.
"I can take off the leg," said Doc Goode, "but
He'll be no use after that." Said Grampa,
"He's never been no goddamn use. Do it."

So, for years thereafter, every eve,
Gran with her cane and Tippy on three legs,
Woman and useless dog walked together,
West, toward the sunset on long days and fair,
And then returned, in cordial company.

❧ *Free Show*

TV killed the free shows, killed them dead.
No more magic summer evenings, Wednesdays,
Doubly magic in that no one called them so,
Not the picture man, his old bread truck
Hauling the wheeled screen hitched on behind,
Racing the sundown over county roads,
Not the farm wives, primping, watchful, quick to
    blush,
Not their thirsty men, not for sure the kids,
Flitting in small flocks, like birds before rain,
Toward a lot at this or that end of Main,
Each used week on week off, to spread the trade
Among the merchants, who paid the picture man
And who didn't call the free shows magic
Either, just good business, give the folks
An excuse to leave off work a little,
Shop a little, talk a little, come to town.
Westerns, bio-pics, Abbott and Costello
Cast their spell on kids and spiraling gnats
While grown-ups moved, tidal, up the street
And down. But no one spoke of charms or blessings,
The same no one who would walk Sycamore's lanes,
Summer evenings, in all the years to come,
Haunted by light dancing in windows,
Flickering like hearth fires, but blue and cold.

Randall Mawer

❧ *Red Man, Black Man*

Grampa flat despised Negro ball players
On tv, which came along just in time
To show them off, especially Cleveland's
Larry Doby, a strong, quiet, angry
Outfielder and power hitter, first black
In the American League, long enough
After Robinson in the National
To be no big deal… except to Grampa,
Who could just barely stomach Satchell Paige,
Shambling, grinning, and pseudo-wise, with a
Windmill wind-up and rainbow curve that made
Folks laugh and miss how he got the hitter,
Which he mostly did, and Grampa approved,
As an Indians fan.
                  But he didn't know
How to feel when Doby plain sassed an ump,
Ran down a fly, broke up a double play,
Lofted a patentedly high home run,
Or rose from the dust after a knock down
To give the pitcher a gaze filled at once
With indifference and the promise of
Certain vengeance. Crackers hated Doby,
And Grampa, never having met a black,
Was a cracker of the crispiest kind,
Blissfully dumb, never to be confused
With facts.
            Grampa saved for me the all-star
Trading cards found under the cellophane
On Red Man chewing tobacco, his brand.

I didn't know till I found a partner
To trade with that he, Grampa, threw away
All black men's cards, thus making them, for me,
Pearls of a price that could not be too great
And of a luster that dimmed my roster,
Eagle-eyed, fleet, sure-handed, lily-white.
So I bartered all I had, or had to,
And did not rest till Doby joined the fold,
And Irvin, Campanella, Newcombe, Mays.

❧ *Mrs. Shellhouse*

Painting by numbers came to fashion, then
Passed as abruptly as it had begun,
And Mrs. Shellhouse had to go clear to
Tiffin for her kits, then to mail order,
Not as satisfactory, catalog
Illustrations being so very small,
And black and white, unlike the finished things
Replicated on the kits' lids—landscapes
(With mills), kittens, poised and glowing still-lifes,
Even portraits of old-country gentry.

Mrs. S adored the choosing, the time
Alone with her art, the finished works framed
(In his basement shop by Mr. Shellhouse)
And ranged on every wall of what she called
Just to herself alone her otherwise
Modest home Best, she treasured that moment
Of grace, when one last touch of the brush point
Obliterated with final color
The final digits and their ovoid blank
And box and brush and tiny numbered jars
Of paint could be cast aside, leaving but
Creation's pride, and dinner to prepare.

❧ *Roller Haven*

Roller Haven was this splendid machine
Whose works we made a part of, wooden wheels
On wooden floors thrumming, sending their thrill,
Their sound, like the hot wire's round the feedlot,
Coursing through bodies drawn taut and atuned,
Our heads cocked to hear, our very fingers
Flexing, feeling the air that passed clockwise
Across them.
                Since, the electric organ
At funeral homes of a certain size
Will take me back, inapropos, to those
Youth Fellowship outings in school buses
Rented for the evening, the chaperoned petting,
The lights spattered from the great globe above,
Wheeling, sliding, also part of the works,
Like the waltzes, the orchid smell, the heat
That seemed to rise up from the floor, all, all
In a quonset hut on the county line,
Ten minutes' ride, ten thousand miles from home.

✺ *Linette Adams*

Bob Adams fought right through to V.E. Day.
After, the train he was on with his men—
Bob was a sergeant—derailed on an Alp
And he jumped. Nobody else did. He died.
They lived. Like Linette, Bob's wife, who opened
Variety and Sundries thereupon.
Five yards wide, thirty deep, and dark, the place
Was a cave, but a pirate's cave, with racks
And counters and little tables heaped with
Toys and party favors and costume jewels
And magazines not to be found anywhere
But Linette's. By the time she'd been open
As long as she'd been married to Bob and
He'd been off to war, she was established.
Boys found the best cap pistols, girls new charms
For their bracelets. Grown-ups thought to honor
Bob, who'd been most likely, with their custom,
And Linette's brave smile let them. Bachelors
Of a certain age tended to loiter,
But Linette knew how to set them down soft
On the pavement just outside a door whose
Bright bell marked egress quite as cheerily
As entering. Little temptation there
For her. No doubt being in trade made one
Hard. No doubt seeing folks all day, helping
With choices however small made one vain.
No doubt keeping quiet about one's luck
Was little to pay to keep it running.

War

It seemed we were forever playing war
Round the Reform Church, whose big trees and bays
And cellar ways furnished ample cover
And which was there for us six days a week,
Better than any park with teeter boards
And swings and other kids' things belying
The pretense of earnest life, earnest death.

The name we used was war, but it was more
Single elimination tournament,
Each against all, to be won by the last
Boy standing. The rules were easily learned:
Scatter like kick the can or hide and seek;
Show yourself, or be shown, and point and fire.
If your cap gun banged first, your foe lay down
And stayed down, an honor-bound spectator
Till game's end. And honor did bind, hooray!
Few were disputes over shots' primacies,
Fewer the signals from dead to living.

Choicest of wonders, there were no complaints,
None at all, from grown-up Reform Christians
Or others elsewhere affiliated.
Did they not hear the crackle of gunfire?
Witness the convulsive dramatics of
Casualties well nigh as pleasing as life
Sustained till loneliness signaled triumph?

❧ *Hardware*

Bolts nuts and nails in bins kegs and pails, and
Washers too and screws. Paint cans all sizes
That boomed when the plank floor gave underfoot,
Which it did everywhere. Galvanized tubs
Big enough to bathe in nearby the stove
On winter evenings. Spools of chain rope wire.
Pans kettles pots mason jars wash-boards knives,
Racks of them, blades slim serrated shaped for
God knew what and old man Mercer, who hid
Back with the kerosene linseed oil drums
Waiting for someone to ask for help so
He could try to sell a left-handed saw
Again, which reminds me of the tools: awls
Mallets and hammers (sledge claw and ball-peen)
Wrenches nested like sardines screw-drivers
Files flat and rat-tailed. Fishing tackle guns
In their locked box glass fronted brightly lit,
The only good light in the store, shotguns
And handguns and rifles—one a Savage
Lever-action carbine, a saddle gun
Like in the westerns. The ammunition
In drawers beneath that box would blow the whole
Damn town to hell in case of fire we knew.

❧ *Arrowhead*

When Colonel Crawford complained of the cold
The Wyandots, ever hospitable,
Built him a fire and tossed him into it.
They found his case for their relocation,
Less than half a battalion strong, wanting,
But in time reconsidered in the face
Of firmer logic and marched to Kansas,
Where they pretty much died out A thousand
Or so "survive" in Oklahoma now.

These erstwhile Hurons, "sedentary" and
Always picking the wrong side—first the French
Against the Brits, then the Brits against the
Yankees—banged from pillar to post until
Crawford found their winter camp on the banks
Of the upper Sandusky and entered
It and history at once. He got a
County named for him, but then so did they,
The Wyandots, and it was they we mourned,
They whose arrowheads we sought, they we made
Our mascots—warriors, braves, and chiefs—
            not soldiers,
And certainly not missionaries, who
Had teased the Hurons with portable organs
And tales of air conditioned long houses,
Of perch suiciding into canoes,
And made, surprising all, some converts
Whose lithographic portraits hang today
In the mission church in Upper, their suits

And high cravats uncomfortable looking
But their black eyes "convicted," so to say.

And every spring, on the Kildeer Plains,
Another plow turns up another flint,
A tiny arrow point cunningly shaped,
And a farmer or farmer's hand gets down,
Rubs up and pockets same, knowing just who
Will cherish it, this best of all trade goods
In the barter economy of love.

❧ *Pesthunt*

Sycamore's war with the starlings and sparrows
Was a holding action until June,
Until the night, the great and signal night
Of all-out assault. Till then boy snipers
Chuffed with their Daisys at sky-made silhouettes
By day, jack-lit the pests under eaves at night,
And propaganda rang from one-by-fours
Nailed broomstick-high and whacked at sunset:
Go-to-my-neighbor's! go! as wheeling cadres
Jabbered and shrieked in joyous reunion
Into the round and perfect maples.

At last, mindful of fouled sidewalks and rumors
Of disease, the masters of law and firearms
Willed the night, the hour, and shotgun volleys
Brought down spirals of leaf and twig and
Delayed but faster falling boneless bundles
Lined up on curbs by boys in their ecstasy,
With here and there in the angle of a beak
A bead of bright blood, lambent in the street light,
Bird song, as it were, silent and distilled.

✣ *Paw-paws*

Paw-paws, pretty good authority says,
Are edible, but we didn't eat them;
We threw them—at birds, trees, but mostly at
Each other. Small, green, and stingingly hard
In the spring, swelling to mushy yellow
In high summer, to boys who had to throw
Something these were the best missiles deep woods
Offered. They grew on weedy little trees,
Whippy, twice or thrice head high, easily
Cropped with hatchet or machete—yes, we
Had machetes, some did, and Bowie knives—
Till just a ring of five or six still stood,
Which, stripped of their branches, could be bunched
     up
At their tops and tied with twine together.
Leafy limbs and chopped down trees made the walls
And roof—we were efficient and far more
Neat here than at home—and the resultant
Green beehive of a hut was camouflaged,
Airy, pleasantly dim, and water tight.
Problem: no smoke-hole drew. But, as it was
Summer, we did not care, sitting cross-legged
In wise council on floor of hut, forest,
Well, *woods*, swept bare and smooth as bum of babe
That each of us had been not too long since.

We built a village of these dwellings, more
Than one per builder, and real was the thrill
When we returned to see them there, splendid

To think what would a stranger make of it,
Tearing past briars, blundering over logs,
Through bogs to see what could be naught but home
To the *other*, there in the greeny shade?

Randall Mawer

❧ *Home Game*

Basketball reigned in Ohio's northwest,
Most near the "Injanny" line, in towns
With schools too small for football, this in days
Before consolidations blurred old grudges,
Old desires, old ways, when the school's brick box
On the edge of town had its own brick box
Of gym attached, this in days when winter
Tuesday and Friday meant just one question:
Home or away?
                Farm boys square and strong,
Town boys lithe and clever, generations
At their backs, set soles a-squeak on polished wood,
Thin clad, sweat in their eyes, midst thump and roar
From bleachers banked high, high under banners
Stained not with blood (not much) nor shot torn,
But sacred still, hallowed in memory.

Reverend Geist (he'd played some ball—
   who hadn't
Played some ball?) wished he could borrow fire
From this altar, wished anyone in town,
Even himself, gave a heart's tithe more
For anything else but this, for *real*
Fast break, four corners, all court press, zone D.
He sucked the likeness like a hollow tooth,
Mindful a moment of a sermon, shrugged,
And went for popcorn, scrambling down the rows,
Hands on friends' shoulders, exchanging smiles
With folk united in a common cause.

Trying on heresy like a new coat
He probably couldn't afford, he probed
How much it mattered what the golden lad
Atop the column locked in the glass box
At the end of the dark hall was doing,
Sinking a deuce or dying for us all.

❧ *Car Radio*

After the game, I'd run to the phone I'd
Scouted out before and call the station.
Fostoria A.M. The call letters
I disremember, as Gran would have said.
But I'd ring, collect, and give them the score,
Then find the Pontiac and drive, waiting,
Listening for this-just-in-from *me.* Meantime,
And after, the music played, the barn yards,
Pole lit, spun past, and rank and file hedges
A darker dark, and woods, the inert towns
Marked by reddish haze on the horizon.
Elvis was there—the dj had some guts—
And Rick Nelson, always underrated,
Not yet dead too soon. Heat rose in layers
From under the dash, the seal-beams spanned dips,
Spoked round curves, and the tires, taking their beat
From road seams, their pitch from the radio,
Sang along with Prudence and Patience's
Only hit: "Tonight You Belong to Me."

❧ *Junior Bogardus*

"Never say die," old Lloyd Bogardus said
Over and over in Junior's hearing,
And writing obituaries Junior
Could not but remember the old man's saw.
So it was "passed," "crossed over," or "expired,"
That last like a subscription to the *Post*,
Short for *Advance and Post*, when someone, well,
Left town in the horizontal manner
And Junior Bogardus had the last word,
Taking some pride in capturing details
And not repeating himself too often.

What with the extension agent's farm notes
And church news and high school sports, the front
    page
Pretty much took care of itself most weeks.
But he never knew and tried not to guess
When he might have to stay past five so no
Bereaved kin or stricken friends would have to
Look at their names (spelled right) a week later
Than necessary. Required, stay he would.

Such was the air breathed by young Bogardus,
Neighbor, citizen, printer, editor,
Junior no more once Senior passed over,
He of blessed memory, dearly missed,
Gone but not forgotten, beloved by all.

✿ *Clint Eckleberry*

Clint Eckleberry was passing clean
And old and getting cleaner and older
Day by passing day, eyes fading from blue,
His overalls too, hair from fair to gone,
Cheeks, chin, lips, earlobes grown bloodless and gray,
Till in the distance Clint was the glint
Of rimless spectacles and shined toe points
Of work shoes—high, black, and well maintained.

Clint could feel himself fading, feel his bones
Soften as color washed out in the
Bathtub, washtub, swirled and gurgled down drains,
To be replaced, hardness and hue of youth,
With recall ever firmer, brighter,
Of mother, of sister grown, of the first
Auto-mobiles, but oftenest of horses,
Their chomp and whuffle and slobber and smell,
The smell most of all, steaming into air,
Seeping deep into skin, clothes, and bootsoles,
Warm smell, brown somehow, blackish brown like
        their turds,
Jack, Handsome, Blessed, Kaiser, all the rest,
Stirring, glancing with frightened whites of eyes
In the stable dark, shying from harness
For the game of it, boosting him from behind,
Drooping in summer's heat, grumbling aloud,
Smart and head up in the winter, hauling coal.

Clint kept the house, awkward rambling shell,
Bright brand new painted, white, but let the barn
Go, bleaching and shrinking in the sun.
There was nothing there, nothing, bits of leather
Cracked and dusty, hanging from rusty nails,
Stalls with beams and bars worn smooth, floors
        stamped,
Embossed with broken bits of curve, of arc,
The mark of hooves heavy and rough shod,
Oh, and the smell, which would remain behind
Long after horse and man and trade had died.

Randall Mawer

❧ *Lett's*

Compromise was not in my mom's nature,
But Lett's Billiard Parlour drove her to it.
I *would* go to Lett's, unless told not to
That day, and if Mom knew I was in there
Because somebody told her when she asked
If I'd been seen—mistake to ask, but then
Mom could be slow, sometimes—I had to be
Gotten out. Problem: gentlemen did not
Frequent pool halls; but neither did ladies
Enter pool halls to collect them. Plan C:
Send an ambassador, a passerby,
Unfortunate soul unless readily
Amused—most were. "Tell him he's needed home."

Mom thought Lett's was evil, and truth to tell
It was as evil as Sycamore got.
No billiards there, just pool, and cards in back,
Euchre the clock around played by old men
Mysteriously never seen to leave
Or enter Cokes. Cigars. Three kinds of snuff.
Chewing tobacco. Off-license beer, but
Not for kids, who weren't there for beer, for sin,
But just pool, the perfection of control;
The planning eye and executing hand
Were all in all. Chance, class, and resumé
Were checked at the door, even brains except
Of a certain sort and brawn to be sure.
And if most winners were the neer-do-wells
Perhaps a kind of compensation reigned,

Perhaps, while we're perhapsing, Mom was right
About Lett's, about sin, about control,
About the strength for ill in self regard.

Randall Mawer

❧ *Chick Starkey*

Chick Starkey yanked out from up in under
Creek banks snakes whose grayish lengths, not lank
    but
Muscular, twisted round his tattooed arm
And whose flat eyes looked back into Chick's, calm
As his own. Chick liked their temperature,
Their slim strength, their assessing regard, liked
These and some few more things: the straight razor's
Whispered rasp across his naked scalp, the
Perfect snap of a muskrat trap, tested
At home before a fresh set tomorrow,
The pin's stab as he made a new tattoo.
Such were the places Chick would fall back to
When his refusal to be curious
About other devices and creatures
Grew too much for the world and it attacked.

Tradition saved Chick, the country custom
Of volunteering as better than jail.
After half a hitch in Korea, he re-upped.
The army thought him just as odd as did
Sycamore, probably, but worked harder
At playing to his strengths. None wore khaki
Better, kept weapon cleaner, stood straighter,
Longer, so that when, the once, Chick came home
On leave and went downtown in spring twilight,
He was a bit surprised, walking the streets
In uniform and alone, to see how
Pretty the town was, and how very small.

Root Beer Stand

It was the little window that did it,
More than the draft root beer, frothing and not
Too cold, in weighty, sweating, manly mugs,
More than the yellowish frozen custard
A bent-tipped cone of which, dunked upside down
In heated chocolate or butterscotch goo,
Donned at once a thin, delectable shell.

Nor was it the everything sauce, with egg,
Hard-boiled and chopped, mixed in, nor the onion,
Chunks of it, dropped on the sloppy joe meat
Of the coney islands, foot long or small.

No, it was the little window did it,
And the new root beer stand prospered until
It was no longer new, and prospered still,
All because of that window, hatch really.
Folks trudged clear from Old Town, or drove for miles
Just to place their orders there, take their food
To a stand-up shelf on the outside wall
Or back to their cars Oh, there were tables
Inside, but that was "sit down," even if
The fare was two hot dogs (with everything),
Fries, and a root beer float.
                              Was the food good?
Why, better than good, if memory serves,
It was grand! As special as a picnic,
But ordinary, too—plain—the food of
Migratory birds, taken practically
On the wing, sufficient unto the day.

Randall Mawer

❧ *Snow Day*

Why is it that the snows of yesteryear
Fell always at night, all memory's storms
Departing with the dark, leaving glisten
And drift behind, a totally done deal?

Yesterday's sun slipped downward like a dime
Tarnished by haze, and wind bumped the windows
Now and again in the night's wakeful times,
But the snow, the snow itself was secret
Even from itself, except where streetlight,
Porchlight picked out the swirl of frozen bugs
Or the first lines of brightness in crevice
Or crack, limning limbs of evergreen trees
Soon to be bending for no eyes to see.

Then the day, and through windows white-pasted
In the corners like album photographs
We saw the storm's nocturnal work at last,
New mountains, new plains, old lines and angles
Blurred and blunted, chimney smoke rising blue
Not gray, the world a tabula rasa
Whereon any boy's chosen course would be
Of consequence, knew school might be canceled.

And choice sang from everywhere: snow angels,
Fox and geese, guidable toboggans and
Sleds or trash can lids spinning where they would,
Snowballs (with forts) if the packing was right.
Money was there to be made shoveling walks,

And those of us old enough to hunt knew
We could read rabbit sagas, and end them.

Soon enough coal grit would descend, darken all,
Tracks of cars, boots would go to slush, harden
Into ankle-wrenching ice, school resume
In the county plows' wake, and the spell fly,
To return only in dreams and memories
(Little to distinguish here) of men old
Or getting there too fast in a world where
Meteorological conditions
Replace the midnight storm *Oùsont les neiges?*

Randall Mawer

❧ *Knut Hofias*

Black was the wind that blew Knut Hofias
Into town, black as his flat hat, blacker
Than the gray-streaked hair over his collar,
Than his rusty suit or cracked dusty boots.
Black was that wind, so said those that believed
The tale of fire in the hobo jungle
Out there west along the AC&Y
The night before his advent, the first day
He walked Sycamore's streets to no purpose
Beyond tipping his flat black hat to all
But especially to wives sweeping steps,
Hanging out wash, standing—why not?—in doors.
No dog barked at Knut Hofias, no boy
But wished to follow him, know whence he came,
Study the bright scarf knotted at his neck
Or his belt buckle big as a saucer.
But the men, oh, the men, going to work
Or coming home, they sniffed at the black wind,
Inquired who fed Knut Hofias, where those
Manners came from anyway, and what kind
Of a name was Hofias, come to that?
Was there no law to prevent a grown man
From burning daylight, holding up a wall,
Measuring shadows, doubtless picking up
Anything that wasn't nailed down? Their wives
Took care not to smile, and their kids, ears cocked
For the warning of the five-thirty freight,
Wondered not at all idly what in town
Was not nailed down, themselves not least of all.

❧ *Jack Ludd*

When Knut Hofias, Sycamore's town bum,
Became a candidate for mayor, Jack Ludd,
Town butcher and mayoral incumbent,
Picked up his steel and made his thinnest blade
Thinner by ringing the two together:
"Any God-damn puddin'head votes for 'm
Deserves 'm," said he. "What's he promisin'?"
(Jack's wife Laureen heard things Jack didn't hear;
Jack had a temper, and a knife at hand,
Always, or a cleaver.) She, surprised at
What possessed her: "He says he'll be full time."
"Full time! God-damn right full time! What else's
He got to do? Sleepin'! Sweepin' out Bragg's!"
"I suppose four hundred a year is lots
To a man like that," Laureen said, Laureen
Who had never gotten used to living
With a man who had blood under his nails
And around them. "I'll tell you just one thing,"
Said the mayor, sighting over the knife's point
At his wife. "He gets one vote more 'n his own,
So help me God, I quit. Not a day more
Will I work for this son-of-a-bitch town!
Not one day more! Shit!" Jack Ludd concluded.
Laureen: "I wish you wouldn't talk that way
When you're handling food."
                              Knut Hofias got
Two votes and soon left town. Jack didn't quit.
But he had to wonder ever after
Who the Judas was, never suspecting
Betrayal night and morning in her kiss.

Randall Mawer

❧ *Dave and Janice Shook*

Dave Shook was mean, no other thing to say,
The way he made his tiny little girl
Of a new wife, Janice, walk behind him
On the berm, all the way to town and back.
She was from Clyde, up around, a cousin,
Some would have it a degree and a half
Too close, corn silk hair, pinkish eyed, bird boned…
Simple, Mrs. Ludd said, who helped her out
With staples in the store, using a list
Dave wrote out. Dave was down in Bragg's just then,
One shot, one short beer, and home, Dave in front,
The girl with her burlap bag three steps back.

Never so much as a word were they heard
To say to one another. *She*, may be,
Never talked at all, not in Sycamore,
Not at the plank-and-horse truck stand she ran
Up on the road there, where Dave's lane came out.
Nobody ever went down to the house,
So run it up out of whole new cloth was
All the town, even Mrs. Ludd, could do
About what went on there in the bow-bend
Of the creek, on Dave Shook's twenty acres
Of sweet corn, melons, peach and apple trees,
Tomatoes, and potatoes new and sweet.

From what they didn't buy, it had to be
They ate their own raising; from what they did
(Fish-hooks and shot-gun shells) some game—oh, and

Eggs—Janice or somebody kept chickens,
Lon Huffman said. (Lon fished down around there
A good deal.) There was interest, always
Interest, but little information.

So if from time to time a big old snake
Slid into their truck patch, interrupting
Their picnic of roasting ears and slabs of
Salted ripe tomato, we had to guess
What Dave did to defend his bride, shoo it
Away or cut its head off with a hoe.

Randall Mawer

❧ *Perce and Hamey's Boy*

Perce and Hamey's house stood close by the road,
So Hamey made Perce keep the shutters closed,
That side, to keep out dust in dry weather.
Inside, the house was all Hamey's, Perce said,
Denying he could keep it on his own,
And he dressed, sat, ate, for all folks knew slept
Like a guest, cleaning up in the wash-house,
Leaving his boilersuit and boots out there,
And his cap, wiping his shoes on the mat,
Tapping the door frame, not to scare Hamey,
Who was almost as nervy as she was
Particular.
        That's why the Clewson boy,
His moving in, surprised the neighbors so.
What would Hamey do with a *boy* rattling
Around the place, kicking the chair legs and
Scuffling the rugs awry, smudging windows?
Still and all, Perce *was* getting on in years,
Not to say failing, and all those acres
In corn, the hogs, the garden and the flowers,
Hamey's flowers but the work was Perce's,
The yard, thick, soft, and green as anything…
Something had to give, and goodness knew
That Homer Clewson wasn't fit to care
For anyone, much less a growing boy,
Once Virgey died, and with Perce a cousin
And all, well…
        Nothing changed around the house.
The boy picked up from Perce what not to do,

Inside, what the field, the stock, the garden
Needed, and if the words passed among them
Were few, and if the screaming of piglets
At castration time echoed in his dreams,
The boy would remember, always, kneeling
On grass like velvet, green as anything,
Weeding a flower border, and Hamey
In silence handing him a piece of cake,
Chocolate, on a china plate, and milk,
And a fork, and an embroidered napkin.

Randall Mawer

✣ *Fishing*

I must not have had my *Plain Dealer* route
Then, if I was fishing in the morning.
An hour before dawn I was up and out,
Night crawlers, their can in a paper bag
To fool my mom, collected from the fridge,
Tackle box in the basket, rod balanced
Across the handlebars, tracking the streets
Damp with dew past houses quiet as death
Out into the right-angled labyrinth
Of county roads to where the iron bridge
Spanned the loud riffle above the first pool.
With just enough light from the east to see
The quill bobber, I baited up and let
The split-shot-weighted rig drift down along
The dipping willow boughs edging the hole,
But one of several mapped in memory
Between the echoing bridge and the bog
Where the creek found the Sandusky River.

Always fish were to be caught, mostly trash—
Carp and suckers, shiners. Bluegill, sunfish,
Sometimes a bass. No crappie this morning.
(It was not maggots I used, remember,
But worms.) And always birds were to be seen:
Kingfishers blazing paths, crying in rage,
Once a great blue heron, called great with cause,
Unfurling like an umbrella, heaving
 Itself into its slow, low flight downstream.
Snakes hung like gray tatters from drooping limbs,

Or swam miraculously, their heads high
And dry. Turtles Deer and fox not unknown.

But it was the creek, mostly, that appealed,
Different in sun and shade, looping wide
Around flat fields and brambly, ugly woods,
Scuffling there, loitering here, scouring
Pitfalls under banks, baring roots' secrets,
Tumbling whole trees into the drink. For why?
All to draw a boy's eye? Boy's heart? Surely
Not. No, the creek's intent was to rehearse,
To train for riverhood, just as the boy
Practiced to be a man, knowing no more
Than the stream he fished in who watched, who cared.

· 47 ·

❧ *Baling*

Creek-bottom grass is hard hay to make,
High, thick, and fibrous from black silt left
By overflow and sucked through matted roots,
Hence hard to mow Hard to rake, too,
Never quite dry, shaded by willows
And hillside. Hard even to reach, down
Switchback track with two-wheeled travois trailer
Banging the hitch. We used the old round bailer,
Lacking space to turn a hitched-on wagon,
Spitting the bales out sideways, big as hogs
And tougher to shift, onto the ground, then
Heaved them onto the ladder-bedded trailer,
Every layer leaving anchoring grooves
For the next, like casks, like green rolls of coin,
To be hauled by the Fordson up and out,
Each load a book, every bale a poem,
With shape and heft and studded with flowers.

Notes

Friends and students with whom I've shared parts of "Sycamore" have found some of my vocabulary opaque and my allusions bewildering. So I decided to provide a few notes, and to take the opportunity to offer a few disclaimers, lest old friends and their descendants see unintended and unflattering resemblances in these poems, which borrow names and, often as not, are pretty pure fiction.

"The Pond"

I did lose a friend to drowning in Sycamore Creek, not in the prototype of Geary's Pond, which is (was?) actually near Marion. The friend, whose death occasioned my first visit to a funeral home (splendid phrase: see "Roller Haven," below), was not at all like Ronnie Esterhaus. The *beans*, of course, were soybeans.

"Social"

The Omar man (genus *bread man*) in his *bread truck* (see "Free Show," below) delivered bread, rolls, and pastries from the Omar Bakery, located I don't know where. There was also a *Tony's man*.

I didn't hear them called *spaetzle* until much later, but that's what they are, those big, eggy noodles-cum-dumplings made by scraping batter off a board into boiling water… or, in this case, chicken broth. *Longhorn* is a mild, rubbery, orangey-colored cheese.

"George Hannum"

There were Hannums in Sycamore. (Donny, the one I knew best, was a clever basketball guard, pitcher and shortstop at baseball.) But George is made up,

borrowing his milkhouse Pabsts, his taste for rhyming verse, and his relation-
ship with his wife from my Grandpa Mawer (on whom see more below) and
his muzzle-loader from Grandpa's hunting companion, the same Reverend
Coleman here called by his own name and (truthfully) charged with his oft-
uttered "I got him!" Both Grandpa and the Reverend lived in my dad's boy-
hood Harpster, by the way, not Sycamore.

A refrigerated *bulk tank* receives the milk either from hand-carried buckets or
milking machine receptacles or, in latter days, through a pipe direct from the
milker.

A *stanchion*, says the dictionary, is half of a set of *stanchions*, upright bars on
each side of an animal's head to keep it in position for milking. Midwest dairy-
men refer to a set as *a stanchion*.

"Mary and Margaret"

Some will recognize the twins as Jane and Janet... now what *was* their last
name? They looked like this all right, but they were perfectly civil... even let
boys join in their girly games.

Hydroxes were sandwich cookies, chocolate with white filling, what a student
of mine not-quite-accurately called "generic Oreos."

"Tippy"

"Tippy," "Tip," and "Tipper" were usually females, unlike this shepherd cross
based on my (and later my grandma's) Laddie.

A *surcingle* is the strap draped over a cow's back to hang a milking machine
from.

"Mrs. Shellhouse"

The paint-by-numbers craze *did* sweep Sycamore when I was in grade school, but to my knowledge none of the town's several Mrs. Shellhouses succumbed to it.

"Roller Haven"

I've renamed "Roller Haven" and moved it: it was more than ten minutes away, way up beyond Tiffin.

A *hot wire* is electrified, to keep stock from pushing through it, and you can, under some atmospheric conditions, hear it hum and sizzle.

"Linette Adams"

My friend Bobby Hosterman lost his dad in the way here detailed. Blanche Ludwig, happily (so far as I know) married to a still-living husband, one of two barbers in town, ran the variety store, here considerably glamorized Blanche was very kind to the paper boys, myself included, who used her shop as a depot.

"Arrowhead"

The quotes are from the *Academic American Encyclopedia*, 1981.

Upper is the almost inevitable shortening of Upper Sandusky, seat of Wyandot County, where the mission church is more than worth a visit.

The *Kildeer Plains* are west of Harpster.

"Pesthunt"

The annual fusillade here described did happen, and boards *were* nailed to trees to amplify the broomstick blows which sent flocks of birds on their way.

Daisy was a brand of air rifle (b-b gun), the only brand I ever encountered.

Jack-lighting is attracting and/or immobilizing game with a flashlight.

"Home Game"

The basketball terminology should be familiar to most: *four corners* is an offensive alignment used (often as a stall) to foil a swarming defense; the *D* in *zone D* is for "defense"; a *deuce* is a two-point field goal.

"Junior Bogardus"

I don't recall the name of the printer-editor of the Sycamore *Leader*, for which I wrote high school sports for a year or two, but it wasn't Bogardus. (I knew a family named Bogard, but not Bogardus.)

"Clint Eckleberry"

Clint lived next door to us and struck me as a kind of a cranky old coot. I use his name, his barn, and his physique; his past I invent.

"Root Beer Stand"

There really *was* chopped hard-boiled egg in the everything sauce.

"Snow Day"

Thanks to my friend and colleague Linda Miranda (see "Meditation," the Baudelaire translation elsewhere in this volume) for help with the Villon quote.

"Knut Hofias" & "Jack Ludd"

There *was* a Knut Hofias, and he *did* run for mayor against the town butcher; but the latter, Ronnie Hosterman's dad and my American Legion baseball coach, did not resemble Jack Ludd.

The *AC&Y* was the Akron, Canton, and Youngstown railroad.

"Perce and Hamey's Boy"

George (not Perce) and Hamey VanGundy raised Hershel Trease, my Uncle Hersh. Their house and yard were always immaculate.

The *wash-house* was the outbuilding where laundry was done, in the days of tubs and mangles. After washers (and later dryers) came in, the wash-house sometimes survived as the place to leave boots, work-coats, etc.

"Fishing"

Maggots really *are* the only live bait for crappie, with their tiny, delicate mouths.

"Baling"

I think I may have invented the term *travois trailer*, after the travois dragged by American Indian ponies and dogs. The wagon rolled on wheels, but only two, at the back of a V whose point rode on the trailer hitch. This wagon was very maneuverable. The *Fordson* was a small, low tractor

Other Poems

Maids' Bower

Here, in the black shade, where vines climb and roses run,
Soon, in the stilly noon, water's marimba tap will come
To call us out, into the glare, across the whitening lawn,
Across the day, away from morn to deeper darkness drawn.
Still poised are we, like birds on wires tugged taut twixt to and from,
Here, in the black shade, where vines climb and roses run.

❧ *I Want To*

Go, like the hurrying crow
Skate-boarding down a bumpy wind
In late November—

Around rocky knobs,
Over bare-bough-banging woodlots
And towns nameless to me,

Across rivers black and green
Stretched taut by the pull of the sea—

And not to care
Where,

Not to foresee, but birdlike
Sidelong glance, not
To define, and with nothing behind

But the wind's push, never
Remember

Randall Mawer

❧ *Noir*

The Hero

Appeals to landladies and dogs, a sign
That not all the little handles he's tried
To file off, bumps the world snatches you by,
Are gone. Withal, he's convincingly smooth.
He likes his hat, snap-brimmed, maybe too much.
Sure that what he is about to do is
Another of those mistakes, he catches
His own eye briefly in the bar mirror,
Shrugs, settles his hat, and turns smiling to

The Henchman,

Who is perforce a bully, a big one,
Noisy, stupid, but self-aware enough
To know he'll be long gone by the last reel
And had better be kicking the pup now
While the kicking's good, prompting the hero
To humiliate him there in front of

The Girl,

No better than she should be (whatever
That means), older than most girls, but classy,
You know? classy enough to show cleavage
In the a.m. and not get arrested.
She and the hero are two of a kind,

And they both know it, but there's this fate thing
They've got to deal with first: he's got a past
(Remember those pesky unfiled handles);
She owes herself body and soul (well, soul)
To the overdressed, slightly older guy,

The Villain,

Who owns the bar, the bully, the whole town
Probably, the cops for certain, and who
Would gladly lose ten years, ten pounds, the dumb
Mustache and play the hero if he could.

Three Sonnets

On the Occasion of a Tree-Planting

by the U.S. House of Representatives Pages,
April, 1990, in Celebration of Earth Day

The more things change, we say, the more they stay
The same. Take trees, time lapsing through the story:
Branch, bud, leaf-blow, fruit, fall. How else know May,
December's wracking chill, October's glory?
But trees *do* change. Glaze of sleet bends, winds bow,
Lightning rives, wildfire turns all to candle.
The seasons' certainty is likewise now
At risk, and we have learned at last to handle
Our world as we would a trout too small to keep,
With hands wet and tender, lest fingers spoil all
And fungus fire consume our children's meat.
Lessons learned late may save this spring from fall.
Suffice it that for now we delve and pray:
Roots, root. Trunk, branch. Give memory its day.

Randall Mawer

❧ *On Attending a Requiem Mass*

For Someone We Didn't Know

Self-righteous habit, Saturday Low: the almost
Empty nave , two candles only, for priest
And acolyte Father, Son, and Ghost
Outnumber us sometimes, so that the Feast
Is quickly kept. Today, though, something new.
The rector fills us in. We check the book
For variations, wait, and wonder who,
And how, and whether, will we, with a look,
Know the mourners, see the mark of loss
Upon them, sense their pain, and understand
Their hope that this is how the flame and dross
Are properly divided, by whose hand?
Most, though, we feel the weight of time to come,
When others we don't know will send us home.

❦ *Ballast*

Stamped with our maker's mark we lie below
The water line, nudging the hull upright.
Where sheets and rudder point us, there we go,
Wrapped in our elemental dank and night.
Base metal in the basement, never gold,
A portable foundation, thermostatic,
Cool in the heat, luke-warmish in the cold,
Most leaden-steady when all above's erratic,
Shiftless beneath the balance edge that we
Create, subduing yaw and smoothing roll,
We gravitate that lighter folk may be
Visible proof of the half-hidden whole,
Content to be the fundamental means whereby
Prow   parts   waves,   masts   stab   sky.

Randall Mawer

❧ *Christmas Exchange*

On the day before Christmas, Christmas Eve day,
After weeks of a winter warm and dry,
It chose to snow, and the flakes spun down
Out of a purple sky.

The warmth of the windows melted them,
But the stubble field to the building's west
Went white at once: this wasn't to be
Another cruel jest

Of Nature's but stuff fit for sleds,
For missiles and forts and who could tell?
For bringing an end to the long school day
Hours before the bell.

"It'll get *bad*, Miss Smith!" we urged.
"The buses will stick in the snow and slide!"
"But what about the Christmas exchange?"
She asked, and our voices died.

(Miss Smith was smart for a first-year hire
And loved by the boys and girls alike;
She was waiting to marry, but in between
She loved her children back.)

So off we went to eat our lunch
In the darksome dining hall downstairs:
Creamed peas with little onions, bread
And butter sandwich squares,

And that day, as a special treat,
Handfuls of filberts heated through
To take to the playground in the snow
For recess until two.

But—glee to tell!—the word went round
That school would close at half past one,
On the word of the cautious principal,
The storm-spooked Clyde VanLunn.

So back we all ran to our class and Miss Smith,
Who thought if we hurried we just had time
To exchange the gifts stacked under the tree
And open them all at her sign.

*   *   *

Here it seems needful to digress
And name two players, boy and girl,
Whose story this one mostly is:
Bid welcome Gitt and Pearl.

Gitt Eustace had been put back twice,
So in year four at Gardena School
He labored still in the second grade.
But Gitt Eustace was no fool.

He, for example, was alone
In his straw-poll choice in forty-eight
Of Harry Truman over Dewey.
It took the combined weight

Of four fifth graders, Republicans all,
Even to try to make him regret

His choice And after the grimmest scuffle
Regret he did not but set

His jaw, wiped his bloody nose,
Taped his broken glasses' frame,
And laughed, as someone not afraid
To stand up for his name

And Harry's. Indeed he was never afraid
Afraid to fight, to fail, to sneer,
And not to care. But we were afraid
Of him, and he knew our fear.

Now Pearl, her last name lost like a button
From memory's coat with time threadbare:
Pearl cried a lot, and wore no socks,
And her hair… oh!… her helmet of hair

Was thick and oily and black as sin.
The very sight of it made us recall
The vermin the nurse was at pains to find
When school began each fall.

So we sang at Pearl to make her cry:
"Pearl, Pearl, she's not nice,"
The cruel ditty ran. "Beware
Of Cootie; she's got lice."

Oh, who would be Pearl? who would be Gitt?
Who even feel in their needful behalf,
In this kingdom where stiffness of heart was the rule
And the motto an ignorant laugh?

   *   *   *

The packages passed down aisle and across,
And all as one at the teacher's word
We tore at the tissue each to find
His or her private hoard.

Inside the wrap of my gift a note
(Did I mention that I was among the we?)
Announced the giver to be Pearl,
And there for all to see

Was a battered box of paints, used paints,
Worn through to the metal beneath them, some.
I could have hidden the gift, the note,
Fate's little jest, all! from

Gitt, who was there, but I did not.
The world's injustice had struck me dead,
As loud enough for the world, and Pearl,
To hear, the tall boy said,

"I wouldn't touch that if I were you."
(I remember the finicky "were" so well.)
"You might get cooties." And then he laughed.
And then we heard the bell

Which summoned us all to the yellow vans
That would take us home through the blowing snow,
Each child to the hearth the gods had willed,
Whether he or she wished to go.

*   *   *

I looked for Pearl where the buses were.
When she didn't appear I went back inside.

An easy sorry burned in my mouth.
I knew where she would hide,

Where she always hid when it got too hard
To stand in the pitiless light that stared
At her ankles bare, her feed-sack dress,
Her black and oily hair.

The classroom was empty, but not quite still.
I could hear her crying there on the floor
Where she always lay when it got too hard,
Behind the cloakroom door.

I kept the door between us, knelt
(I must have looked like one at prayer)
And pulled from my pocket, my right hip pocket,
The hankie my mom had put there

That morning, two quarters tied in one corner,
To buy paper and pencils and soap for the poor,
For kids in the city, our pen pals that year.
So there on the classroom floor

I knelt in a kind of prayer, fumbling
For the coins Miss Smith, confused by the snow,
Had not collected, placing them side
By side on the floor, just so,

And sliding them into the dark. "Pearl,"
I said, "here," and got up and left the room
And the school behind for the long walk home
Into an early gloom.

So it was that once on Christmas Eve,
After weeks of a winter warm and dry,
It chose to snow, and the flakes spun down
Out of a purple sky.

Randall Mawer

❧ *Litany in a Time of Transpiration*

… [P]eople seeking help need to provide some information about their own faith journeys. God communicates with each of us in a way that is unique. The more fully we can delineate patterns of God's communication over the span of our lives, the more effectively we can evaluate what is transpiring at the moment.

—*Listening Hearts: Discerning Call in Community*

So, just what *is* transpiring,
At the moment?
The wind, oh!
Through the window,
Bellying the cheap fiber screen,
Then on, into, through
Heart; sweat, through
Skin, cloth, into
Air again.
Cycles, vicious and other,
Everywhere cycles:
Food chain, clouds bearing east,
Tri-, bi-, uni-.
Who
Rides on three wheels in the morning,
Two at noon, and one
At the circus?

What is transpiring?
Puns.
God never scruples to pick a
Pocket,
So
His Sphinx is ever at the
Gate,
Riddling us,
Rat-a-tat-tat, but
We

Have twenty carrots planted
In our ears and can't
Hear the words.

Poor, helpless metaphors,
Dying, dying, dying.

Faith journeys diverge in a yellow wood,
And I?
I took the low road,
Seeking Dublin,
But when I got
There,
It was a disappointment. Two stars.
Some language
Inappropriate
For children.

I am the way
(That is unique,
In fact,
Very unique),
The truth,

The life.
Jesus (he was a handsome man)
Said that,
And…

If you want to talk about a span,
Man
(Life included)
Give me a tall horse to measure,
Or (better yet)
Give me caissons, pylons,
Verrazano Narrows, Cabin John, Mackinac,
And Hart Crane staring
Astern.
Give me a
Wherefrom,
Whereto, and a
Tollbooth,
For God's sake.

And, hey, do they mean "delineate,"
Sketch out,
Draw lines (in the
Sand), or
"discern"
(Cf. title), *see?*
What you see is what you
Get, I guess, and
This book was written by a
Committee, and committees have a
Cow, man, or a
Camel, maybe Joe, and
Would you walk a mile

(In my shoes) for one,
Or not?

What is transpiring is
What I read in "Calvin and Hobbes."
What is transpiring
Is
Language,
The gift of tongues,
Stuff
That
Breathes
(Never transpires)
The breath of life.

In its light
We see light.
Lighten our load,
Light up our
View from the ditch/slough/drain
/Gutter
Whereby stands
The tired, good, patient
Samaritan, reaching
Down past his filthy ankles
To lend a
Helping hand.

Help us to do unto others,
Help us to be done unto *by* others
Gracefully,
As if
Filled with
Grace.

Four Tales

❦ *The Green Man*

The Green Man came walking, ten feet tall,
Out of the west, the sun at his back.
No bindle, no staff or cane,
Nothing bulging in his pockets.

All this we saw and agreed about after.
But we disagreed too—about the color
Of his eyes, his hair, his beard,
Whether he *had* a beard even,
And what he wore on his feet.

Miss Margaret Kitchin, our oldest neighbor,
Leaned over her gate and addressed him:
"Green Man," said she, with little to lose,
"Do you have something for me?"

"Perhaps on my return," Miss Kitchin said he said,
In a voice that was pleasant,
Sweet even, and young, though his face,
His green face, was scarred and wrinkled and worn.
"And his eyes were sad," she said.

"What color were they?" Worthin the cobbler wanted
    to know.
"Blue, I think," the spinster said, "blue
Like the morning glories. Yes. Bright blue."

"Did he say anything else?" But no, he hadn't.
He climbed the long hill out of town,

Heading east, stopped just the once, looked back.
Some said he waved. I didn't see it.

He hasn't come back And if he does,
Bringing something for Miss Margaret Kitchin,
He won't find her, because she died,

Died, her friends say, whispering of green hands,
Of strong green arms below rolled up sleeves,
And eyes of morning glory blue.

❧ *It Was the Cat that Stayed*

Not many talked to Jasper Klegg,
But those that did advised him
He was wrong to court the gypsy girl.

He was too old, they said,
And set in his ways, and she was young
And, after all, a gypsy.

But Jasper, when he thought things through,
Remembered his mother, who had always
Welcomed the travelers to the elm grove

On their visits, not more than one a year,
Believing that their only crime
Was to be different, and proud.

Jasper's friends, if friends they were,
Might have spared their pious breath, for the girl,
While kind enough, would not have him,

And when, that last night, Jasper walked
Down to the camp with a chicken
For a gift, the travelers were gone.

Nothing remained but smoking embers
In the fire hole and the cat,
A skinny gray thing with one green eye,

And one gold, which followed Jasper home,
And stayed, and kept the place clean of rats,
And went with Jasper to the field,

The barn, even to town, sliding
Quick and stealthy from tree to tree.
The rare visitor to Jasper's place

Might find the cat on the farmer's lap,
But it—*she* to Jasper—soon
Moved off if the company stayed at all.

Nothing else changed, oh, except the gypsies
Never returned to the county and
All of Jasper's barn cats ran away.

❧ *Grandfather's Spectacles*

Before he could even walk, the golden glimmer
Of Grandfather's spectacles drew his baby's eye,
Baby's hand "You can have them when I'm gone,"
Grandfather would say.

And then he *was* gone, and the boy, walking now,
Watched them lower the box down, there
In the churchyard on the high bluff
Over the river.

And he was very sad but did not speak,
Spoke, indeed, not at all. "Take him with you
Fishing," Mother said, and Father did,
For quite the first time,

Tying him by a short rope to the gunwale,
Talking to him the day long, off and on,
Drifting down river and back up on the tide,
Having splendid luck

The whole time! In the shadow of the high bluff
Father pointed to a cave mouth halfway up
And told the story—could it be true?—
Of the orphan prince

Who lived once in the church cellar.
"There was a tunnel so he could run,
They say. That could be the tunnel."
The boy said nothing.

But he heard. And when he went missing
And the boat too, Father had a suspicion,
And it was not long before they found the boat
Tied up to a tree

Below the cave and the boy, knees and elbows
Skinned but not really hurt, not sick,
Not even frightened, really, but smiling,
Just inside the cave

And headed out. He was speaking now, again.
His mother thought perhaps time had had its way,
And the new love of the father.
It could have been true.

Or it could have been what he hid and brought back
From deep inside the hill, which he never spoke of,
Never showed his whole life long, and what he saw
When he looked through them.

❧ *"Don't Send Me Dreams"*

"Don't send me dreams, old woman," Robin said.
"I've carried your wood and water now, so if you
Please, don't send me dreams."

"Don't call a person old," the red witch said.
"I was at school with your mother. And its plans,
Bad plans bring bad dreams."

Robin had seen a giant snake in the cistern,
And monstrous births, waking the family
With his yelling. "What bad plans?"

"How could I know?" the woman said.
"Take these." She pinched a leaf, two leaves
From a weed by her door.

"Burn them in a bowl at bedtime.
Sniff the smoke." Was it pity made the gift?
"Come tomorrow, do the chores,

I'll give you breakfast." And Robin hurried on
To the orchard, where he worked the day
Away side by side

With pretty Elizabeth, not so much
As smiling and careless with the ladder,
Leaning in his mind

Toward the dark. "How old is the red witch?"
He asked at supper. "My age, about,"
His mother said.

"No, younger. And don't call her witch.
She'll know, even if it's only in your head."
The leaves burned that night,

And Robin rose up lightly, having dreamed,
Could he remember, of a leaping sea
And purple hills above.

He ate with good appetite
The meal the woman give him,
Slipped onto his finger

The ring he found at the bottom
Of his cup, silver it was, and went
On his way.

And the red witch grew younger
By a day.

❧ *Aboard the Skipjack Sigsbee*

The jib cracks in a wind flaw.
Otherwise silent as under sail we
Tack,

And the boom swings round
And the eye is drawn
Up. See
The off-white sail cloth
Belly.

Lungs fill like the sails.
No land-smells here.

Little waves dance.
Hearts dance.

See
There, no there, to starboard, see
The schooner, just there,
Three perfect sails
Under the fat black guns
Of the green, green fort.

See
The *Lady Maryland*
Racing the merry wind
In the clear gold noontide light
Of May.

Randall Mawer

❧ *Perfect and Getting Better*

She waxed more comely in every way
Each day, and all who saw pronounced it true
She knew. None bespoke her, but every eye,
Though shy, held up reflection to her view.

Too did she see herself in her own glass,
This lass no longer, vainly essaying,
Weighing one merit against all the rest,
The best to choose, no rude haste betraying.

Visible virtues none beside claimed she:
Envy touched her soul for one standing by
Whose eye could comprehend the whole of her
As 't were in one glance with no mirror nigh.

Love she had heard about, an idle thing,
The king of lesser province than her own,
Alone among the principalities
To please with blossoms not quite fully blown.

Bawmer Orals

Randall Mawer

✣ *Scoring From First*

The O's played on tv last night,
And in the bottom of the fifth of a scoreless tie,
Harold walked—Harold Baines, the dh, forty,
Number retired already in Chicago
But still going
On knees that are simply gone.

Anyhow, the Twins pitcher had a no-hitter going
When Harold worked his way back from oh-and-two
To get the walk, and then Conine drove a spike
Into the gap in left center and the ball
Skipped clear to the wall and you knew,
You just knew Harold would have to try
To score all the way from first. "Run, Harold, run!"

The voice was mine, and loud,
Loud enough to drown the rasp
Of the bare bone balls in bare bone sockets
Of Baines's ruined knees as he cut the corners,
Sharp, at second and then at third,
Where the base coach's arm wind-milled like crazy
As the relay man wheeled and threw home.

Baines scored standing up, and the Twins pitcher was
    rattled
And the O's picked up another run
And Erickson hung tough
And the Birds notched a win, pretty if meaningless.
They're out of the race, and so are the Twins.

But the standings didn't matter to Harold
Any more than the pain he hid—always hides—
Behind a half-smiling mask.

What matters, to Harold and me and you, if you're lucky,
Is that he laid off one more younger man's hard one,
Just too high and probably unhittable,
Read the angle and arc of still another liner
Off another teammate's bat, and read it right,
Hit two more bases with the inside foot, and crossed
      over.

Oh, and one more thing which matters to me
And would probably matter to Harold if he knew
(He seems like a very nice man):
When I yelled at him, at the tv screen,
It was my father's voice I heard,
Which Harold would have heard if I'd been at Camden
      Yards,
Loud and urgent, and singularly happy.

I sounded just like Dad. "Run, Harold, run!"

B.J. Surhoff, the Baltimore Orioles' all-star left fielder, goes through a unique ritual just before he enters the batter's box, and sometimes between pitches. He holds his bat vertically, almost at arms' length in front of him, business end up, and stares intently at the sweet spot, just above and a quarter turn to one side of the trademark. Sometimes his lips move a little. I have often wondered

❧ *What B.J. Says to His Bat*

No, this isn't just something I do to get focused,
The way some of the guys fiddle with the strings
    on their batting gloves
Or cross themselves or twist the handle two ways
    at once.
Wilbur says I'm looking for hits in there, and he's
    close to right,
Pretty close.
The thing of it is,
It's not like fielding or throwing or running the bases,
Where you just watch the guys who are good
And listen to coaches and think and drill
Until you get it right
And then drill some more.

Hitting isn't like that.

Oh, sure, I work at it
In the cage and at the tee, till sometimes my hands
    blister and bleed.
But that's not getting ready to hit, exactly.

That's just paying the price.

Maybe some of the guys hit the ball with their bats,
Maybe… they don't talk about it,
Talk about everything else, but not that.

I don't. And I know I don't.
You do it And if I've paid the full price
I can *let* you do it,
No push or pull, not so much as a twitch.
You go get it, I watch
And stay the hell out of your way.

That's how it gets done.
Every time, it's a miracle.
And being a miracle, it might be the last. So,

I promise never to say anything else.
I promise never to think anything else.
And I swear, if that son of a bitch
Jams me and saws you off just above my hands,
I may have to pick up a new stick,
But so long as I live, by the sight in these eyes,
I will remember you.

Randall Mawer

On Seeing Natalie Portman

In Ted Demme's Beautiful Girls Close on to My Fifty-fifth Birthday

If she stopped for a tick
She'd freeze stock still.
(Think Grecian urn.)

So stop she doesn't but
Dances like flame across
A landscape ugly
With ice. She stomps snow,
Shoves sled under side porch,
Fidgets, sidles, and, best,
Skates, round and round
The squalid pond, graceful
And gawky betimes.

"[A] set of two or more
[E]quations, each containing
[T]wo or more variables whose
[V]alue can simultaneously satisfy
[B]oth or all,"

She moves

And prattles—book smart,
Street smart, just *plain* smart.

Thirteen years old.
Unlucky thirteen.

No wonder the guy,
Cupping cold hands
Round the candle's flare,
Doesn't want to settle.

(Sure Timothy Hutton's too old
For the part. Who isn't?)

Randall Mawer

☙ *For Study and Discussion*

"In the first stanza, what do the birds follow that the motorcyclists
can't find?"
—re a Thom Gunn poem, *Adventures in English Literature,*
Heritage Edition

Multiple choice:
(A) bugs, (b) a map, (c) their leader,
(D) "their instinct, or their poise, or both"
(Gunn).

And, while we're on this patch, other
Mysteries:

What does the dogwood know that the latch-
Key can't turn?
The voice intone that the hard
Drive can't eat?
The kiss that the thimble abhors?

Their instinct, or their poise, or both, or
Neither.

Wait.
Do not pass go, do not collect

Any amount, or seek admission to the Wharton
School, do
Not Please Until
The big, hairy, helmetless guys on Harleys
Uncover what it is which
The birds follow, until
They stop to smell the dogwood,
Warble country songs, kiss
The girls without making them
Cry. Then, poised instinctively
On their hogs, loud and low-slung, on
They may go…and we may ride
Along.

"Would You Baptize an Extraterrestrial[?] and other theological questions posed to the Jesuit astrophysicists of Specola Vaticana"

—*New York Times Magazine*

Like, hey, have you seen some of the specimens
We've got in the pews already?
Is this a gift horse,
Or what?

"'When you look through a telescope, do you see
Cold gases commingling
Indifferently or a coherent universe
Governed by a loving God?'"

Third hypothesis, to wit:
That not all gases, albeit, to all
Appearances, cold,
Are indifferent about
How they commingle,
And with whom.
"Coyne is not just a respected astronomer… who…
Can call Stephen Hawking a friend."

One does wonder, though,
What Stephen ("the mind of God")
Hawking calls Father Coyne.
George? (Probably George.)
"[T]he Guaicuro Indians
Had no word for resurrection....
Kino stunned some flies and
Then let them stir
Back to life....
This fits in...
With my idea
Of Jesuits."

Mine too. As flies to wanton priests
Are we to the gods.
They stun us for their sport,
Then let us stir
To instruct the savages. Meantime,

"Father McCarthy leans forward.
'Angels,' he whispers,"

Are extraterrestrials believed in by Jews,
Christians, and Muslims. But do angels
Believe in Jews, Christians,
And Muslims... and/or distinguish
Among them?

"The astronomers believe that man
Can move in on nature and
Work out a deal, even in the can-
Opied forest of the red squirrel....
'How,' I ask, 'can you... find...

Comfort in the contemplation of a
Gravitational constant?'"

Well, says Stephen Hawking's probably-
Not-so-very-good friend,
God is in the data.

❧ *Meditation*

Be good and keep still, oh my Pain.
You were calling the Evening to you; it descends; here
    it is:
A dark air envelops the city,
Bringing peace to some, to others cares.

While mere mortals, the vile multitude,
Under the whip of Pleasure, that tormentor without
    mercy,
Will clean up the remains of servile celebration,
My Pain, give me your hand; come over here,

Far from them. Watch how they hang out the dead Years,
From the balcony of the sky, old fashioned dresses;
How smiling Regret roils up from the bottom of the
    waters;

How the dying Sun falls asleep under a bridge's span,
And, like a long shroud trailing off to the East,
Listen, my darling, to the sweet Night, stealing away.

—Charles Baudelaire
tr. with Linda Miranda

Randall Mawer

The Sargent Show
at the National Gallery

Adorable children swathed in fat,
Palpable dimples borrowed from Cassatt,
Just down the hall. A bug-eyed matron
Wondering about her gown. (An apron
Would be mas naturale.) The fortunate few
Twinkle, in on the joke, to wit, who
Would remember us lacking the "treatment"?:
Diabolique, little me, downright, meet me
Later. The master, meanwhile, more concerned
With background—lambent lilies, lantern
Light, olive boughs, shadows, implications—
Till all is irony, and big commissions.

❧ *It's a Joe*

Some of my ties are a bequest
Of sorts from J's mom's dad,
Wide things, and shiny, and now back
"In," it seems.

The kids I teach, who know designer
Labels (though never heard of the Trojan horse)
Finger the one with the blue
Elephants or the jack-straw-patterned one
And ask, "Is this a so-and-so?"
And I say No,
It's a Joe

Hesley.
His rooming house dresser was found
Stuffed with shirts, pajamas,
Still—in both senses—unopened,
Still be-pinned, be-cellophaned.
What do you give a man who has everything
He needs?

They went at yard-sale, those wrapped-up gifts,
Toward his last month's rent.
But people would know
The ties, we guessed, and,
Superstitious, might not buy.

So I got them
And wear them, and smile at my enigma:
No, it's a Joe

Hesley,
Deft railroad tinsmith,
Maker of toys and laps and old, old jokes,
Moving silent, mostly, and sure along the very
Outer orbit of a system whose
Solar heart
Is love.

❖ *Listening for Ghosts*

Only people have abandoned the spot,
This hilltop lower than other hills around,
Left it to weeds, cloud shadows, and the sound
Of wind and quite occasional rain, not
So much lost as never fully caught,

Even by those who rest under these stones,
If rest they do, their names and dates falling
Away, their thin voices finished calling,
Imploring those like them now merest bones,
Who answered if at all in thready tones

Blown away by the perpetual past,
Leaving not even an echo behind,
So that all now are one, the harsh, the kind,
Swirling and slanting in the wind, the last
Sound before the door of earth is locked fast.

❧ *Dybbuk*

I met myself today, walking
In sun glare down an old street
In an old town by a wide river.
His hair was thin, thinner than mine,
His eyes were lighter in a darker face,
And the pinky of his left hand
Was gone to the second knuckle,
The stump end taut and shiny.

He didn't seem surprised, so I
Stayed cool as well, looked him over
Lightly, made to offer him my hand.
He ducked his head, shook it a little
I think, and dipped from his shirt pocket
A sheet of paper, folded thrice,
Passed it, and moved on The poem read,
Of course, "I met myself today…"

www.ingramcontent.com/pod-product-compliance
Lightning Source LLC
Chambersburg PA
CBHW031312060726
47590CB00003B/1178